For Bernard Naumburg
these old lines — I've checked a few
I commend still, gently — with best
wishes
William Meredith

March 1972

See contents

Corrections p33
p39

SHIPS AND OTHER FIGURES

A PUBLICATION OF THE

J. FRANK RUSHTON MEMORIAL FUND

OF PRINCETON UNIVERSITY LIBRARY

SHIPS
AND
OTHER FIGURES

BY WILLIAM MEREDITH

PUBLISHED FOR THE PRINCETON UNIVERSITY LIBRARY

BY PRINCETON UNIVERSITY PRESS

1948

FOR

Charles and Josephine Shain

CONTENTS

ENVOI

Go, little book. If anybody asks
Why I add poems to a time like this,
Tell how the comeliness I can't take in
Of ships and other figures of content
Compels me still until I give them names;
And how I give them names impatiently,
As who should pull up roses by the roots
That keep him turning on his empty bed,
The smell intolerable and thick with loss.

CARRIER

SHE troubles the waters, and they part and close
  Like a people tired of an old queen
Who has made too many progresses; and so she goes.
Leisurely swift her passage between green
  South islands; careful and helpless through the locks;
At lazy anchor huge and peacock vain.
On the streaked sea at dawn she stands to the streaks
  And when her way and the wind have made her long,
The planes rise heavy from her whining deck.
Then the bomb's luck, the gun's poise and chattering,
  The far-off dying, are her near affair;
With her sprung creatures become weak or strong
  She watches them down the sky and disappear,
  Heart gone, sea-bound, committed all to air.

TRANSPORT

Now seven days from land the gulls still wheel
  High and astern. Quiet but fierce with hunger
They follow the fantail: so does the violin, steel-
  Thin, follow a high voice in desire and anger.

Her slow stern rolling to the sea, the ship
  Travels with no bird's blessing, and burns her waste.
Bird and hull describe the rise and dip
  Of heavy ocean where there is no trust.

I think I know a new myth and this is it:
  The strength having gone out of certain old men,
    Formerly terrible, they are changed to gulls
And follow over endless ocean hulls
  Of their rejecting states, wishing for them
    Catastrophe. But we shall prosper yet.

BATTLEWAGON

I SEE you standing out from the mind's roadstead
For nowhere, as like as not, and moving dimmer.
White and greys that shake along your side
Would disguise you as volcanoes or as nuns,
But although the cut steel pieces of your guns
Drop together like a puzzle I would never have patience for,
And though below decks, terrible with valves, containing
    war,
You are as baffling as a motive for evil,
I know your profile like a first lesson.

Old Billy-be-damned bang bang flashy-in-battle
Castle not obsolete with turrets grinding deep
Into chambers of oh by jesus noise,
All for one or at most a few battles.
The rest of your years readying you go
Up and down the inappropriate blue
(Because nothing remembered, nothing faraway).
Your crew and tackle exquisite with purpose,
I see you standing off the heart's headland
As like as not for yesterday, and I wave.

A FIGURE FROM POLITICS

THE gigantic sweet conspiracy of lovers
Who had once thought to take over everything
Will now, I am convinced, come to nothing:
Right about race and Russia, we were wrong
When it came to local affairs touching each other.

"DO NOT EMBRACE YOUR MIND'S
NEW NEGRO FRIEND"

Do not embrace your mind's new negro friend
Or embarrass the blackballed jew with memberships:
There must be years of atonement first, and even then
You may still be the blundering raconteur
With the wrong story, and they may still be free.

If you are with them, if even mind is friend,
There will be plenty to do: give the liars lessons
Who have heard no rumors of truth for a long time
But have whatever they hear on good authority,
Whether it concerns Chinese women or the arts.

Expose the patrons, some of whose best friends
Are brothers, and who are never now anonymous:
What kind of credit do they expect for that,
Ask them, or better, ask their protested brothers,
The grateful tenants who can't get their curtsies right.

Finally the injured, who think they have no friend,
Who have been convinced by the repeated names
That they are jews or negroes or some dark thing:
They must be courted with the lover's touch
And as guiltily as if yourself had turned them inward.

· 6 ·

If you complete this program, you will have friends
From all the rich races of your human blood:
Meantime, engage in the often friendless struggle.
A long war, a pygmy war in ways,
But island by island we must go across.

DEDICATORY POEM

Who cannot tell for certain
　The short love from the true,
Or cloud from faroff mountain,
　Or faraway from blue,
　What can I promise you

Except that form's compulsion
　And truth's will hold me firm
Against other persuasion
　Until these lines grow warm?
　And you are truth and form.

BLUES

I was driven by love but my lover hung out No Parking,
I was ridden by fear that my lover would post away,
And it happened, and now I don't mind remarking
That today is the bluest today is the bluest day.

Say, is there repose in the purlieus of lover's sorrow
And a car-port to park in without backing and filling?
If there is I'll purchase a home there tomorrow,
Live within my means with a girl moderately thrilling.

I'm through with running a taxi for a while
That love can whistle for everywhere I cruise;
I'm going to ride around this town in style
And sing the organized lovers' blues.

MIDDLE FLIGHT

THE loneliest place I know of nowadays
Is a cumulo-nimbus cloud I seem to find
As often as I fly; I went there first
When the sky and a war were new, but memories now
Are as heavy in its belly as a squall.
It is a tall cloud, something gathered at the tops
But opening to imprecision, at the base to rain,
And the hope that it held five years ago is spilt.

But what I mean to say about the cloud
And its forlorn vicinity where gather
Vapors of doubt that not our lonely day
Shall see precipitate, is that even here
Nobody goes alone who knows so much
As one human love; so much I know,
Whence hope, if any, in the covered sky,
Choir in this uncompanionable air.

AGAINST EXCESS OF SEA
OR SUN OR REASON

THE sea that comes to the beach now softly
  Like a woman giving a gift,
Has taken at night whole fields, and in winter
  Has pitted the sentry cliffs.

The sun that turns your body to wanted brown
  Has tricks to make men black
And can bleach from bone of you the offending flesh,
  His glancing changed for a long look.

The warm and honest mind, the heart's keeper
  And body's hope of innocence, knows a quirk
To cause repeated error in choice of friend or lover
  And put an end to work.

RECONVERSION SONNET

We write at Christmas now who watched all night
From choice on Yeats and freedom or from need on war,
And are no longer quite agreed what for
We kept those watches and some of us died.

Now war is altered from the work we shared:
Less active than our waiting and less brave
It is a neurosis men and nations have,
Some lacking will, some counsel, to be cured.

The freedom that we watched has moved across
The seas and hills ahead like any star
And fixed or clouded tells us we are far;
And Yeats, as we have moved, means more or less.

Across these changes knowledge does not yearn
To innocence, and we cannot return.

LINES WRITTEN BUT NEVER
MAILED FROM HAWAII

No one is snug against the heart's disasters,
Not the men and women that I know;
(The learned and the loved that went along
Ate their knowledge and their beauty like a drug)
And of disasters, absence may not be the worst;

But the things I could tell you about sunrise in the islands,
About the sense of summer troubling the cane,
Of flight as smooth as love above the sea at night
—I have looked at the ocean in moonlight for a long time,
But no more than death's meaning can I say what it means—
The things I could tell you while the sun declines
Of the gentle play of mountains on the mind;

For absent lover ever and be certain that for me,
These seasons were disasters, these times of day.

THE IMPRESSMENT

DAYS like today we are the clouds' men
And what they do all day is our concern.
Taken with their success and clean-edged march
Against the sky in rout, we join up;
The moon recruits too on certain nights
When the clouds run before, bellied or enfilade.
But tented strangely later we wish ourselves free,
Seeing the cause false and us poorly led:
The authority of clouds is mirror-practiced,
Their maneuvers are pieced out by espionage
From the discarded dome system of the sky,
Their military secrets are all useless data
For secrecy's sake kept, for an air of mystery.
And clouds do not take into account the mixed duties
To anyone's invalid father, troth to a cripple,
Or an old borrowing, kept in peacetime mind
And asking payment; do not reckon,
In other words, on the complicated day
That anyone wakes to the sky blank blue or grey.

STRING QUARTET

(FOR RANDALL AND MARGARET THOMPSON)

I

How learn our way among these mazy strings
Who wander lost all modern afternoon
Used to the lazy harmony that sang
Last century dear archaic tunes?
Effortless the velvet cello moved
Through troubles easy to anticipate;
The violin in love was always loved
By the viola pretending to be late.
The almost-discord, lightly overpowered,
Removed like a foiled villain to the wing
When virtue's exquisite motif appeared
Singing a tune that anyone could sing.
But though we cock a critically-tuned ear,
These novel troubles are our own we hear.

II

"Never again the same" declares the cello,
"Nevermore" the sweet viola, and "No more"
The second violin, "No more" the first.
"It is our peculiar nature" they all say
"To make a foolish and a sweet lament."

"Things were luckier then" recalls the cello,
And the viola: "Those were the halcyon days,"
"It was well then, it was very well then,"
The violins recapitulate; then the first:
"But I can languish, I know how to yearn
For festivals remembered of old loves";
The strings below, diminishing, in turn
Brag of imagined luxuries removed.

"Never again the way it was before,"
"Never again, although we bow it far,"
"However fair today or seeming fair,
Never again, no more, no more, no more";
"It is our peculiar nature" (the song went)
"To make a foolish beautiful lament."

III

SMALL comfort the creepy cello nowadays;
Its intervals contrived against repose,
It questions everything the violins say.

There seems no place for simple early praise
Among the dangers that these strings expose;
Small comfort the creepy cello nowadays.

Have we outgrown the gracious rondelay,
And, too-late-born, the fancy of the rose,
That we must question what the violins say?

There is real danger in the sterile way
That sets apart the poem from the prose:
Take no comfort in the cello nowadays,

Mistrust this modern dissonance they play
As either too cerebral or a pose;
I question everything they have to say

Unless perhaps our dissonance today
Defies all resolution; unless, who knows
—Small comfort the creepy cello nowadays—
The question lies in what the violins say?

HOMERIC SIMILE

As when a heavy bomber in the cloud
Having made some minutes good an unknown track;
Although the dead-reckoner triangulates
Departure and the stations he can fix,
Counting the thinness of the chilly air,
The winds aloft, the readings of the clocks;
And the radarman sees the green snakes dance
Continually before him in attest
That the hostile sought terrain runs on below;
And although the phantom shapes of friendly planes
Flit on the screen and sometimes through the cloud
Where the pilot squints against the forward glass,
Seeing reflected phosphorescent dials
And his own anxious face in all command;
And each man thinks of some unlikely love,
Hitherto his; and issues drop away
Like jettisoned bombs, and all is personal fog;
Then, hope aside and hunger all at large
For certainty what war is, foe is, where America;
Then, the four engines droning like a sorrow,
Clear, sudden miracle: cloud breaks,
Tatter of cloud passes, there ahead,
Beside, above, friends in the desperate sky;
And below burns like all fire the target town,
A delicate red chart of squares, abstract

And jewelled, from which rise lazy tracers,
And the searchlights through smoke tumble up
To a lovely apex on some undone friend;
As in this fierce discovery is something found
More than release from waiting or of bombs,
Greater than all the Germanies of hate,
Some penetration of the overcast
We make through, hour upon uncounted hour,
All this life, fuel low, instruments all tumbled,
And uncrewed.
      Not otherwise the closing notes disclose,
As the calm, intelligent strings do their duty,
The hard objective of a quartet, reached
After uncertain passage, through form observed,
And at a risk no particle diminished.

CIVIL TWILIGHT

THIS may be the time and these free forms
　　Of cloud may be the colored clouds I mean;
The long light on the lawn is right that warms
　　As the angle lessens, and gilds that green;
The ridge that lifts between the sun and here
　　Relates now gradually to the trees in space
And to the houses heretofore too near;
　　This may very well be the place.

This truce of dark might settle once for all
　　The differences between the parts of earth.
　　　　All day I have predicted such a rite
Where indecision topples like a school
　　And the hostile halves of all admired faiths
　　Take harmony before the fall of night.

A BOON

WHAT I will ask, if one free wish comes down
Along with all these prodigalities
That we pick up like dollars in a dream,
And what I urge you ask, is not that we
Grow single in our passion without gap,
Losing with loneliness dear differences;
Nor lust, to burn a lifetime resinously,
Although that surely were a miracle
Worth asking, and a project for two saints,
Feeding themselves by bits into the smoke.
No, let us more ambitiously demand
What I'd go lonely and unpaid to hold,
The power I've heard the bravest lovers have,
Really to aid and injure one another.
Whereas there's no security, in dreams
Or waking, of the things we need the most,
The risk itself cries out to be possessed.

WEDDING SONG

(FOR LOUIS AND EDITH COXE)

Sweet friends that late in June remove
Into your private unity,
Trying the generosity
Which we protest who love you both,
May every gay and sober trick
Known to your seasonable retreat
Attend it, and that chief lovers' luck,
That solitude at last be cured.
The image is of healing here:
The body of affections—how
Fragile it remains at last—
Takes wounds that drain the mind though hidden,
Wastes whole years at games indoors,
And can be sutured only by part and part
Touching as you have done.

Never childhood nor the sea
Nor anything you can't describe
Come between you in the day,
Nor across your utter rest
Be effort to communicate,
Even though the event shall prove
Self-conscious lovers really to be the best.

Opening without suspicion
Every secret door,
Show your late impenetrable keep
From the uppermost pavilion
Where the gulls and Sisters sweep
To the loose place in the floor
Where a shoddier alternative
Was once provided for.

Be the love you make at night
Lightly lightly humorous
A gentle parody on love,
And though they may be bitter jokes
Private jokes divert you two
When conferences are called on man
That even irony sits deadpan through.
Although we live in niggard years
When faith is listed critical
And patriots go light on hope,
Feast we you deserving pair
On our last stocks of red belief.

Such private grandiose art be yours
As purges public tragedy,
And lovers' art be seen for art enough.
By your new cleverness inform
—If form, as we believe, can save—
The systemless and headline world
With the whole aesthetic lovers have:

Beauty is when two lovers really meet,
Or where the symbol comprehends the thing,
Or it can be if a system is complete;
Lover to lover in every part is sweet,
And image to imaged thing from head to foot,
And nothing surpasses total anything.

IN A COPY OF YEATS' POEMS

Accurate knowledge was prerequisite:
He set the Coole swans at fiftynine,
Knew by sight the mackerels' teeming habit
And tried to learn whole curved philosophies.
Now sidewise like a dusty stroke of sun
His figures and the figures' meaning stream.

GIFT POEM

The roads are full of ships that tug at anchor,
The fields hold rows of shiny idling planes,
That might lace up the salt or high degrees
That gape between us separate where we sleep.
Your longitude and latitude read: amorous;
The winds that blow from that quarter now are spiced
With all the invitation spirit can extend
To spirit or blood to blood; in which air
The duty I wait on seems a thin necessity,
And without virtue that high-spoken hero
In the conflict of love and duty
Who never chooses love; in which warm air
The thing that does not wither in the hand
Is love and more particularly your love.

TWO FIGURES FROM THE MOVIES

I

The papers that clear him tucked in his inside pocket
And the grip of the plucky blond light on his bicep,
He holds the gang covered now, and backs for the door
That gives on the daylit street and the yare police.
But the regular customers know that before the end
With its kissing and money and adequate explanation,
He has still to back into the arms of the baldheaded man
With the huge signet-ring and the favorable odds of surprise,
Somehow to outface the impossible arrogant stare,
And will his luck hold, they wonder, and has he the skill?

II

PERICLES:
This is the rarest dream that e'er dull sleep
Did mock sad fools withal: this cannot be.
My daughter's buried . . .
O Helicanus!
Down on thy knees, thank the holy gods as loud
As thunder threatens us: this is Marina . . .
Mine own, Helicanus;
She is not dead at Tarsus, as she should have been . . .

THEY wouldn't dare to let it end like this:
Her lying still and silver on the screen.
Surely some recog ~~recog~~ recognition scene   w M
Will cornily restore our stone-dead child,
Her who for reels beguiled us and who lies
Now mirror-undetected and called cold.

THE DOUBTING SCHOLAR

WHERE is my scholarship who used to hold
In the small of my back the warm feel of the sea
From September to June again, not cooled
By coasting days, and in my nostrils the smell
Of grandmother's drugs between biennial visits?
Rages now of ocean are not recalled
Betweentimes unless written down, or the feel
Even of love, in my latter-day research,
Though I the more lover today take further to mutable sea.

What findings can the forgetful scholar reach?
In notebooks names alone of the cryptic great
Are legible in this short light, remind
That here enthusiasm used to study
But left his books to go live with a loss.
Wordsworth at thirty, Spender's disabuse,
Were half the dulness that unmemories me:
One small conviction toppled like a school
And all the town around fell powdered down.

POET'S VIRTUE

No IMAGE takes me from you, being there;
The usual swan, the catalogue of flowers,
Keeping their proper essences and powers,
Are only in their functions like you fair,
And I like bird and blossom virtuous there.

Apart, I look for something to compare,
But metaphor in all the idle kind
Offers no purchase to comparing mind
That would scale up or descend from you sheer;
No image takes me to you, being here.

Here speckled fowl sit pointless on the flood,
The plants are hybrid by a driftless breeze.
Idleness is where no poem is
And must be this country. I err abroad
That can live virtuous only in your servitude.

THE BELLS

THEY were convinced their love would last, because
They had met each other real, not conjured
By special needs into lovers' likenesses.
He knew her somewhat wise and partly good,
She saw him lovely planner weak to build.
And it did last, but this was their dismay
—Not equal to their love, but still severe—
That nightly, though their loneliness was gone
And though they wanted no one else, they knew
Descend around them separately two bells
Of glass, set in a rubber base and pumped
Of air until no sound would carry between.
Then in their bells seeing each other fondly
They found they could not speak until day broke.
The bells they came to know their limitations,
And that only the great, of course, can greatly love.

AN *UBI SUNT*

Somewhere between the time that I decide
And starting, is where I hear the past,
Seductive as the sailor-luring sea,
Singing come-all-you's. And then it seems
That I once was dazzled and danced with
Many a fair field of folk, that the things
I was included in then were far and away.

The fact is, no fell so rocky bleak,
Enterprise or love so weary thin,
But the singer past will turn a taking phrase
Making them foreign and the heart's.

It seems there's no forgetting.
Shaking the head, refuse to be bemused,
The chanty chorus still calls after,
Its long interval in the ear, its places somewhere.

THE FELON

All that I value was come by by theft:
Flicker-out talents, long walks with the great,
Some lightning insight into the machines
Of art, of certain lovely ones their love.
If on the deathbed of my youth I confessed,
Restored what was unspent, foreswore my friends,
Took service or enlisted in the world,
Could I go straight now? No, the lottery is fixed,
I see my man coming this way with the number,
And I whom money will ruin will be filthy rich.

WHY SO MANY LOVE POEMS?

A FEW short lyrics should tell all of this
But it runs on and on. You may well ask
How many times be taken by love-in-the-eye,
Its fustian predictions, promising anything?
And ode on ode on love in the doubtful proof,
Whose big images rove as smooth as hands
But never can be named, quick and probably wicked.
For instance: her parents duped, in May,
He lies on one elbow until painful dawn
Where she not-to-be-known sleeps deep—
No sonnet matter, but for part of him fatal;
And all June or longer a kind of wandering
Wherein he is uncertain what *that* was.

If in a stanza some love goes beyond
The merely sung to keep its promises
Or break, I do not know that love first hand.

A BIRTHDAY EXERCISE

> Why leave out the worst
> Pang of youth? . . . To be young means
> To be all on edge, to be held waiting in
> A packed lounge for a Personal Call
> From Long Distance, for the low voice that
> Defines one's future.
>
> —W. H. AUDEN

Suppose I were to take you blindfolded
Or drugged asleep or sleeping naturally,
So that all where and when and most of who
Had left you, and you opened five new senses
To an amber croquet-tocking afternoon:
Strange parasols and fowl confront you now,
You hear their whir, and blazered tenor laughs,
The new terms *shandygaff* and *dead on Joan*.
Grass smell and canvas in the dozing air
Melt in the mint-sweet glass cool people bring,
Parent, but unfamiliar and all rich;
While chiefly through the sky an errant sun
Now flies its certain circle to go straight
Into the endless post-meridian blue,
Diminishing so slowly you can't tell;
Nor will the pigeon-eddied stable clock
Ever say bed- or ~~any~~ any time at all.
Wouldn't you know, however strange the props
I set you, wouldn't anybody know,
Strolling the summer afternoon I made,

That you had been impressed in the hard ranks
Again of children?
               But I would only try
The figure for its currency, to see
To what extent these things are general,
Not leave you there, knowing what I know:
    Everything the years do
    Can be called a kindness
    And what lies behind us,
    Howsoever candied
    By the memory,
    Has for only virtue
    That it lies behind.

PERHAPS THE BEST TIME

O waly, waly,
But love is bonny
A little while when it is new,
But when it's old
It groweth cold
And fades away like morning dew.

—ANONYMOUS

This would be spring, if seasons could be found
  In everything; or if times, this would be morning.
  We dazzle at this first warm shy half-turning
As at a sunrise or at quickening of the ground.
There leafs along our boughs what would astound
  Old botanists and set dead lovers yearning—
  And yet October will see all this burning:
I know because I stay here year around.

We flourish now like Theban royalty
  Before act one: right now Delphi seems far,
    The oracle absurd. But in the wing
Is one who'll stammer later out of pity
  —I know because I've seen these plays before—
    To name his actions to the fatal king.

ACKNOWLEDGMENTS AND NOTES

MOST of these poems were written and all of them collected while the writer was a Woodrow Wilson Fellow of Princeton University, and particular acknowledgment is made of the liberal provisions of that fellowship. Publication of this book was financed by the J. Frank Rushton Memorial Fund of the Princeton University Library.

Some of the poems in *Ships and Other Figures* have previously appeared in *Furioso, Poetry, The Sewanee Review*, and *The War Poets*, an anthology edited by Oscar Williams.

NOTES

The following notes are offered to the reader who cares to use them, for three purposes:

1. to define or explain special words and usages, many of them of military origin, which are not generally known.

2. to identify references, where such identification is essential to the meaning of a poem. Thus it seems legitimate in *The Doubting Scholar* to tell what is referred to in the line

Wordsworth at thirty, Spender's disabuse,

because the line is not self-contained, and the reference cannot, in a sense, be completely understood in terms of the poem itself. On the other hand, no identification is supplied for the borrowing from Chaucer in the first poem or for the borrowing from *Piers Plowman* in An *Ubi Sunt*, because the recognition of such references is pleasurable, if at all, only to someone already familiar with them, and is not essential to an understanding of the poem.

3. to solve syntactical ambiguities. This seems to me a useful and legitimate kind of annotation. The nature of the language and the methods of poetry frequently result in ambiguous construc-

tions in English poetry. In such cases, where a clear indication of the primary meaning is not given by the context (as in the last line of the *Wedding Song*), an explanation seems the right of the reader. I recall with gratitude the light shed for me on the first line of Shakespeare's eighth sonnet—"Musick to hear, why hear'st thou music sadly"—by Dyce's note: "i.e. Thou whom it is musick to hear, why hearest thou, &c."

The writer does not believe that this kind of annotation is a confession of inadequacy in the poems themselves, nor does he intend to add by the notes anything essential to the poems which they do not already contain.

Carrier: l.5. "locks"—the locks of a canal.

ll.7-9. A carrier normally launches her planes only when she is under way and proceeding upwind, so that both her motion (or 'way') and the motion of the wind have the effect of increasing the length of the take-off run down the flight deck. The wind makes streaks in the direction of its movement upon open water.

Transport: l.3. "fantail"—the stern of a ship where it flairs out above the waterline.

l.6. In wartime, to avoid detection by enemy submarines and aircraft, ship's waste is burned rather than jettisoned at sea.

Battlewagon: ll.3-9. The purpose of camouflage of large ships is not primarily to make them difficult to see, but rather so to obscure their characteristic structural features in profile as to make them difficult to identify as to type and number.

Middle Flight: A connotation that the writer would like this title to convey, but is too remote, is the negative of Milton's grandiose phrase in the invocation to *Paradise Lost*:

> I thence
> Invoke thy aid to my advent'rous Song
> That with no middle flight intends to soar
> Above th' *Aonian* Mount. . .

Lines Written but Never Mailed from Hawaii: l.7. "cane"—sugar cane.

Homeric Simile: l.6. "clocks"—a term used colloquially for all flight instruments, as in the phrase 'on the clocks' for 'on instruments.'

l.7. The commonest type of aerial radar screen shows land masses as green wriggling lines, and (l.11) airplanes as "blips," large or small flickering spots.

l.33. "uncounted"—in aerial dead-reckoning, elapsed *time* is a chief factor, and must be known at all times.

l.34. "instruments all tumbled"—gyroscopic instruments are said to tumble when excessive flight angles or manoeuvres unbalance the gyroscopes by exceeding their extreme angles of operation, or when the gyroscopes cease to revolve at operating speed. The readings of a tumbled instrument are meaningless.

Wedding Song: l.27. "Sisters"—the Pleiades, daughters of Atlas, who were metamorphosed into doves and placed among the stars.

In a Copy of Yeats' Poems: ll.2-4. Although I should not like to rule out others, my particular references for these three lines are: *The Wild Swans at Coole, Sailing to Byzantium*, and passages from *A Vision*, respectively.

l.55. i.e. no thing surpasses that which has totality or any system that is complete.

Gift Poem: l.1. "roads"—roadsteads, anchorages.

l.10. The reference is a general one, to the hero of French classical tragedy.

The Doubting Scholar: l.15. The Wordsworth poem I think of here is the Ode, *Intimations of Immortality from Recollections of Early Childhood*, especially the early stanzas. The Spender poem is no. XIII, "What I expected," from *Poems*, London, 1933.

An *Ubi Sunt*: John Edwin Wells, in *A Manual of the Writ-*

ings in Middle English, says: "The 'Ubi Sunt' formula . . . has well been said to be 'as universal as the themes of mutability and mischance'; it has been utilized both in humorous and in grave literature from the Far East to America, and from before the period of Classical Greece to the present generation. It was a special favorite of mediaeval writers."

l.4. The Come-all-ye is an English, Irish or American ballad (and doubtless may be of other nationalities), characterized by an introduction or refrain of those words. Many sea-chanties (l.14) are Come-all-ye's.

Perhaps the Best Time: l.5. "leafs" is a verb.

ll.9-14. The sestet of this sonnet refers to the story told in Sophocles' *Oedipus the King*. Oedipus, now king of Thebes, had been told by the oracle at Delphi that he was destined to slay his father and to commit incest with his mother. The gradual disclosure to Oedipus that he has, almost innocently, fulfilled this destiny forms the dramatic structure of the play. The herdsman who reluctantly reveals to Oedipus who he is and what his relationships and hence his actions have been, is the character referred to in lines 11-14. "His" in the last line thus refers to the king.

But these references can be taken as to tragedy generally, I think, without knowledge of the play referred to.